way to crocHet!

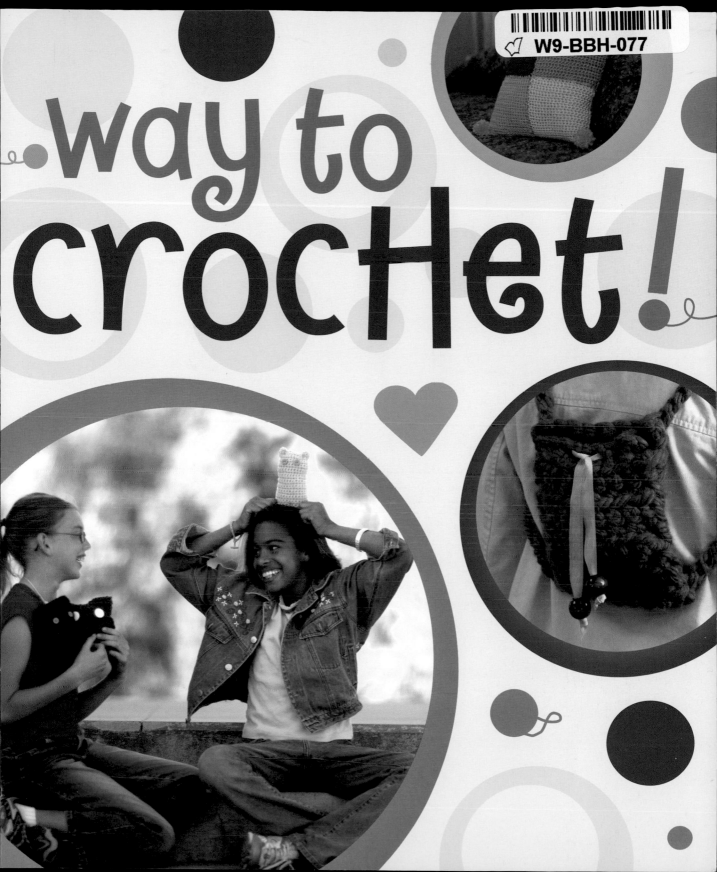

way to crocHet!

20 cool, easy projects for KIDS of all ages

Sherri and Michelle Haab

Watson-Guptill Publications / New York

acknowledgments

To Dan, for the great photographs, and to Rachel and David for all of your help.

Thanks to all of the great kid models and many thanks to the editorial and design staff at Watson-Guptill for their dedication to this project.

Senior Acquisitions Editor: Julie Mazur
Editors: John A. Foster and Anne McNamara
Designer: Margo Mooney
Senior Production Manager: Ellen Greene

Text and photographs copyright © 2006 by Sherri Haab
Photography by Dan Haab

First published in 2006 by Watson-Guptill Publications,
a division of VNU Business Media, Inc.,
770 Broadway, New York, N.Y. 10003
www.wgpub.com

Library of Congress Cataloging-in-Publication Data
Haab, Sherri.
  Way to crochet! : 20 cool, simple projects for kids of all ages / by Sherri Haab and Michelle Haab.
      p. cm.
  Includes bibliographical references and index.
  ISBN-13: 978-0-8230-1053-0 (alk. paper)
  ISBN-10: 0-8230-1053-8 (alk. paper)
  1. Crocheting—Patterns. I. Haab, Michelle. II. Title.
  TT825.H25 2006
  746.43'4041--dc22

                        2006012453

Printed in China

First printing, 2006

1 2 3 4 5 6 7 8 / 13 12 11 10 09 08 07 06

MEET OUR FABULOUS MODELS!

Aisha Brown

Megan Garn

Ayesha Gulley

Chloe Harlan

Hailey Harlan

Courtney Headman

Courtney Lafevre

Megan Larsen

Keilara McCormick

Sara Ripley

Bryn Starkey

Kylee Udy

Tessa Weight

...and Gimli, our adorable dog model!

contents

best-friend bracelets

stuff to make!   30

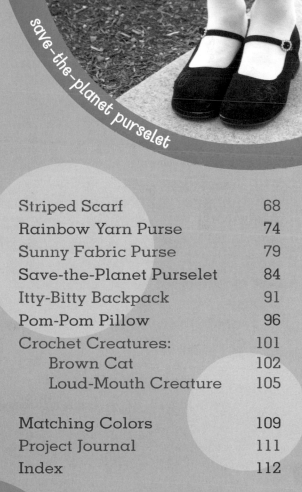

save-the-planet purselet

striped scarf

introduction
why we love crochet!

SHERRI SAYS...

now is the perfect time to learn how to crochet! It's easy and fun, and with so many great yarns to choose from, even a first-timer can make tons of great stuff. All you need to know is a stitch or two to create great projects for you, your friends, your pets, and even your room. The best part? These projects are small enough to take anywhere! All you need is a ball of yarn, a hook, and a bag to hold them in. You can crochet on the bus, on long car rides, at a friend's house—wherever!

From jewelry to belts, cat toys to stuffed animals, there's something here for everyone. All of the projects are simple to do and require very little yarn or other materials to complete.

The patterns are based on just two stitches: chain stitches and single crochet stitches. It's easy! Before you know it, you'll be crocheting squares and rectangles that can be transformed into scarves, purses, pillows, and more.

And guess what else? You can crochet with other things besides yarn. We'll show you how to use fun materials such as ribbon yarn, strips of fabric, and even plastic bags!

We hope you have fun on your adventure into the exciting world of crochet. I guarantee you'll be **hooked** in no time, just like we are!

Sherri Haab

MICHELLE SAYS...

my mom and I have done crafts together for as long as I can remember. The first time I crocheted was when I was about 6. My grandma taught me how to make Christmas ornaments by crocheting around a wire to make a Santa head. I remember how much fun it was to hang my ornament on the tree and to know I made it myself! Now that I've been crocheting for a while, I like to try and make my own designs. Sometimes it works out well, sometimes not so well. Like the time I tried to make a winter hat and ended up with lime-green leg warmers instead!

There are so many cool things to crochet beyond hats and leg warmers. This book is all about projects that are easy and fun to make. You can use any type of yarn, although if you're like my mom and me, you'll love hunting around yarn shops for new glittery and bright-colored yarns! It's so much fun to start with a ball of yarn and end up with a great project—like a bracelet to wear, a cute purse, or a funny stuffed creature to call your own. I hope you enjoy the craft of crochet as much as we do! Have fun!

Michelle Haab

what you need

believe it or not, all you need to start crocheting is a hook and some yarn! On the following pages, we'll tell you about the basics and fill you in on some extra tools that are good to have around, too.

yarn

nowadays, there are tons of yarns to choose from in almost any color you like. There are solid colors, multi colors, and even stripes! Yarns are made from natural fibers like wool, cotton, and silk, and some are made from synthetic fibers, like acrylic yarns. There are also new, special yarns, called "novelty" yarns, which include fancy metallic and shiny ribbon yarns.

Yarns are described by their **weight**, or thickness, which can range from super fine (the thinnest kind), to medium, to super bulky (the thickest kind). For the projects in this book, you can use any yarn you happen to have lying around! If you do decide to make a switch, try to pick a yarn that is the same weight as the one listed. Here are just a few common types of yarn used in this book:

* **Worsted weight** yarn is a medium-weight yarn. A common type of this yarn is the acrylic yarn you can find in most craft and knitting stores in a variety of colors. It is easy to crochet with and very inexpensive.

* **Sport weight** yarn is a tightly woven yarn that is slightly thinner than worsted weight yarn.

* **Cotton yarn** is smooth and rope-like. It is less fuzzy than acrylic yarn and very easy to crochet with.

A SOLID BEGINNING

When getting started, it's a good idea to stick with a solid-colored yarn, because the stitches will be easier to see and count. An inexpensive acrylic yarn is a good choice when you are a beginner.

* **Wool** yarn is sturdy and rich looking. It is more expensive than acrylic or cotton yarns.

* **Bulky yarn** is extra thick and can be crocheted with jumbo-sized hooks. Because the yarn and hook are big, you can make a project very quickly.

* **Novelty yarn** is made from unusual materials. A good example of novelty yarn is ribbon yarn, which looks like flat, skinny ribbon. Other novelty yarns have glitter, fringe, or metallic string woven into the yarn.

* You can also crochet with things besides yarn, like fabric, elastic, string, and even plastic bags! It's fun to experiment and create unusual and exciting crocheted fabrics.

Yarn is sold wound up into balls or "skeins." For small projects you will only need one skein or ball of yarn. When buying more than one ball or skein of yarn, first check the paper label to make sure you are buying yarn from the same "dye lot," which means the colors are the same. Also check the yarn label for suggested hook sizes and care instructions.

WHERE'S THE END?

When starting to use a new skein, pull the yarn end from the *center* of the skein (you may have to dig around a little). This will help keep the yarn from knotting and twisting while you work.

Yarn comes wound in balls (like the red one below) and skeins (like the purple and yellow yarns below).

crochet hooks

a crochet hook *is* the tool you use to make loops in the yarn. It looks like a little stick with a hook at the end. Crochet hooks can be made of aluminum, plastic, or wood, and come in a range of bright colors. You can buy them in any craft, sewing, or yarn store. Most of the projects in this book were created with an inexpensive aluminum or plastic hook.

Crochet hooks come in lots of sizes. The thinner the yarn you're using, the smaller the hook you should use. (And the thicker the yarn, the larger the hook.) Hooks are marked in millimeters (mm) or with a letter of the alphabet to indicate the size. Sizes are listed from smallest to largest, so an "F" size hook will be smaller than an "H" hook.

Sometimes—if you're using a really, really thin yarn, like thread—you'll want an even smaller hook. Steel crochet hooks, or "thread" hooks, are marked with numbers. Unlike yarn hooks, thread hook size numbers are listed from larger to smaller, so a "7" hook would be smaller than a size "00" hook.

Pictured below are different sized crochet hooks. A light blue yarn needle is on the very bottom.

GET HOOKED!

a good idea when you are just getting started is to look in your local yarn or craft store for an inexpensive kit containing an assortment of hooks in different sizes. This way you'll always have the hook you need!

needles

You will also need yarn needles and sewing needles to make your crochet projects.

Large blunt-tipped yarn needles are good to keep on hand with your crochet supplies. Yarn needles have a large eye (opening) on one end and a blunt tip on the other. The larger eye makes it easier to thread the needle with yarn. The blunt tip allows the needle to pass smoothly through crocheted rows without snagging the yarn fibers.

Yarn needles are available in plastic, which makes them both affordable and yarn friendly.

In addition to yarn needles, it's good to have a few sewing needles around, too. These are helpful when sewing materials, such as buttons or embellishments, onto a project.

other supplies

Here are a few other supplies that are good to keep in your crochet bag:

* Good pair of scissors (look for scissors that come in a case to protect yourself from getting jabbed by the tips)
* Ruler or tape measure
* White fabric glue, or Fray Check (found in any craft store)
* And don't forget a roomy bag or a basket to hold everything in!

getting started

now that you've got your materials, it's time to start crocheting! In this chapter we'll show you how to do the basic stitches, from getting the yarn on your hook to starting your first row, and, finally, finishing it all up.

what is crochet?

Crocheting is the process of connecting loops of yarn with a crochet hook. You build rows of loops on top of each other, and this creates a crocheted fabric. You can create crocheted fabric in any shape or size. In this book we'll start with small projects that you can do quickly and easily.

The first real step in any crochet project is to make a **foundation chain.** This is your first row of stitches. A foundation chain is made up of **chain stitches,** which are loops that are linked together.

Once you've made a foundation chain, the next step is to start working **crochet stitches** into the chain stitches, one after the other. When you've finished one **row** of crochet stitches, you turn the work over and start on a new row. Think of it as laying bricks, row upon row, to build a house.

A **pattern** tells you exactly what to do to build your project. It will tell you what kind of yarn to use, what size hook to use, and how many chain stitches to put in your foundation chain.

Crochet uses a hook to connect loops of yarn. You build row upon row to create a crocheted piece.

BE PREPARED

always take a minute to read through the entire pattern before starting a project. Do you have all of the materials? There's nothing worse than running out of yarn when the stores are closed! Do any of the steps look confusing? If so, practice on a scrap piece of yarn first. That way, you'll be all set when you start making your project.

start with a slipknot

first you need to attach the yarn to your crochet hook. You do this by making a slipknot. These instructions and photos are for a right-handed person. If you are left-handed, simply reverse the instructions, switching the left hand for the right hand in the photos.

1 Make a loop about 6 inches from the end of the yarn.

2 Bring the working yarn (the yarn coming from the ball of yarn) up through the loop, making a second loop through the first.

3 Hold onto this loop while pulling the working yarn and the 6-inch tail. This will begin to tighten the first loop, making a slipknot.

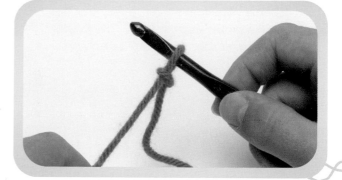

4 Insert your crochet hook into the loop you just made and pull until the loop is snug around the hook. Don't pull too tight; leave a little bit of room so the hook can slide.

holding your hook

now it's time to get comfortable so you can start crocheting! The first few times may feel pretty strange, but it won't take long before you get the hang of it. Here's how most people hold their hook and yarn. Remember, these photos show a right-handed person. Just switch the hands if you're left-handed.

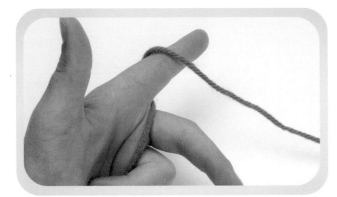

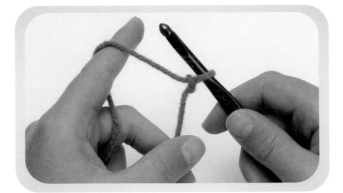

1 Wrap the working yarn (the end that connects to the ball of yarn) over your left index (pointer) finger, as shown. Bend your fourth and pinky fingers into the palm to hold it. This keeps the yarn taut and even as you work.

2 Now pinch the hook with your right hand. Slide the fingers of your left hand close to the hook and slipknot. Use your left thumb and middle finger to pinch and hold the free end of the yarn. As you crochet, these two fingers will move along close to the knots on the hook. (Watch where these fingers hold the yarn as you follow the photos in this chapter.)

FIND YOUR STYLE

this is just one way to hold the yarn. Some people prefer to loop the yarn over two fingers (index and middle finger) instead of just the index finger. As you begin to crochet, you will find what works best for you.

making chain stitches

Once the yarn *is* attached to your hook, the next step *is* to make a foundation chain, which *is* made up of chain stitches. A foundation chain *is* the basic start to any crocheted project.

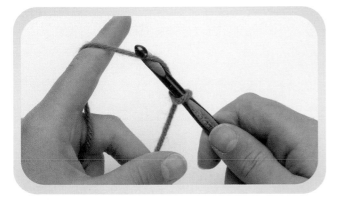

1 To make your first chain stitch, bring the hook under the yarn so that the yarn is wrapped over the hook. This is called **yarn over**.

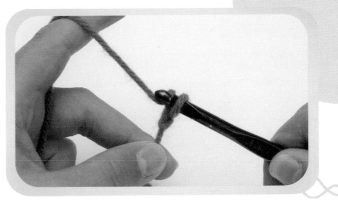

2 Pull the yarn down through the slipknot loop on the hook, pulling it all the way through.

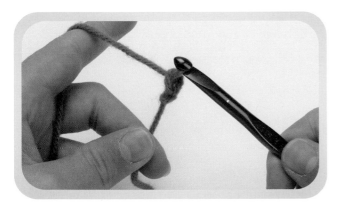

3 Congratulations! You've completed one chain stitch! (Notice that we don't count the slipknot as a stitch.)

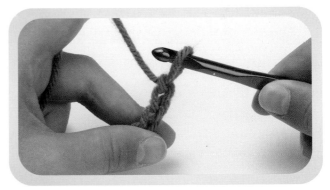

4 To make more chain stitches, repeat steps 1–2. Each time, bring the yarn over the hook and pull the yarn through the loop on the hook. Count each stitch as you go. This picture shows a few stitches.

making single crochet stitches

after you have made a foundation chain, you are ready to begin your first row of stitches. In this book, we will only be working with the most basic crochet stitch, called the single crochet. Even though the single crochet stitch is easy, you may feel a bit clumsy working your first row. It's not your fault—there are just fewer stitches to hang on to! Things will go more smoothly as you move along.

Before beginning your first row of single crochet stitches, look at the loops along your chain row. You will notice that the loops on one side look like a series of Vs. Each V has a top loop and a bottom loop. You will be inserting your hook under the top loop of each V stitch.

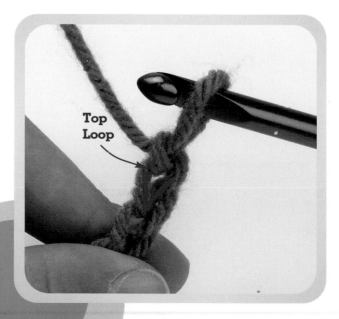

Top Loop

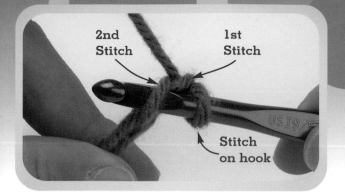

2nd Stitch   1st Stitch

Stitch on hook

1 To begin a single crochet stitch, insert the hook into the top loop of the second stitch from the hook. (Don't count the loop on the hook). Slip the hook into the second chain stitch. Look at the stitches in the photo above to know which stitch to insert the hook into.

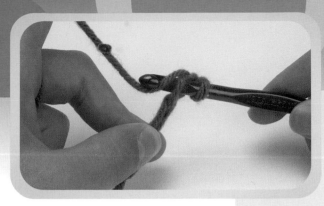

2 Hook the yarn (yarn over) and pull the yarn through this chain stitch. The yarn is only pulled through this stitch, *not* the loop on the hook.

Now you have two loops on the hook.

3 Hook the yarn (yarn over) again.

4 Pull the yarn through *both* loops. Remember to keep the yarn loose; don't pull too tight. You have completed one single crochet stitch! This would be counted as stitch number 1 of your first row.

continued on next page

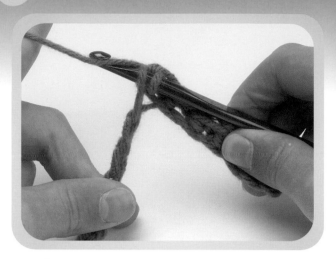

5 Now you'll just repeat steps 2–4 to make single crochet stitches all along the chain. Remember to make a single crochet stitch in each of the chain stitch loops along the row. Steps 5–7 on this page show you the stitch again. Keep repeating this stitch until you reach the end of the row.

6 Do a yarn over, then pull the yarn through the chain stitch.

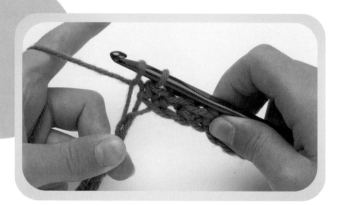

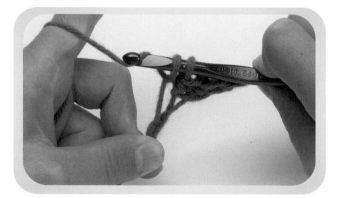

Now you have two loops on the hook.

7 Yarn over and pull the yarn through both loops. This completes another single crochet stitch.

STRAIGHT ON

it's important not to twist the chain as you work. Keep the chain stitches facing the same direction, so that you can clearly see each chain stitch. Remember the stitches will look like Vs.

8 Complete the row with a single crochet stitch into the last loop at the end of the row. This stitch is the first chain stitch you made when you started. Notice that you do not crochet into the slip knot (this will appear as a tight knot at the very end of the row).

9 At the end of the row, crochet one chain stitch. This is called the "turning stitch." This is done at the end of each row every time. It will keep the number of stitches the same for each row. Yarn over and pull through the loop on the hook to make one chain stitch.

COUNTING ROWS AND STITCHES

When counting stitches, always count the first stitch after the loop on the hook. Do not count the stitch on the hook as a stitch.

1st Stitch

2nd Stitch (Insert the hook in stitch #2)

starting the next row

reat, you've finished one row!
Ready for another?

1 Flip the work to your other hand. For the second row, you will be working on the *back* side of the first row. You're going to slip your hook into the stitch marked on the photo. This is the last single crochet stitch you made on the first row. Now it will be the first stitch of your new row.

2 Slip your hook *into* both loops of the stitch. The second row of single crochet stitches is very similar to the first row, except this time you insert the hook into the two loops on the top of the row.

3 Yarn over and pull the yarn through the first stitch on the row, under the two loops of the stitch.

You now have 2 loops on the hook.

4 Yarn over and pull through both loops this time.

You have completed the first single crochet stitch on your second row.

5 Continue crocheting a single crochet stitch into each chain stitch, following steps 1–4 above. Keep going until you reach the end of the row, then make a chain stitch before turning the work over to start another row. You're crocheting! Keep doing rows, just like this last row, back and forth, following the pattern. Count your stitches after every row to make sure you always have the right number.

> "My best friend is the one who brings out the best in me."
>
> —Henry Ford

NOBODY'S PERFECT!

One of the best things about crocheting is that if you make a mistake, all you have to do is pull out the stitches and start over again! You can pull stitches out as far back as you want or need to go. Then, simply insert the hook into the loop you pulled back and start crocheting again. Wouldn't life be great if all mistakes were this easy to fix!

finishing

When you are done crocheting a project, there are a few final steps before you are absolutely done. Once you learn these easy finishing steps, you'll have all the building blocks you need to create all sorts of great stuff.

FASTENING OFF

To finish your work, you need to fasten off the yarn so it won't unravel or come undone.

1 Cut the yarn about 6 to 8 inches away from the last stitch.

2 Hook the yarn and pull it all the way through the loop on the hook.

3 Pull the end of the yarn tight to finish.

HIDING THE ENDS

After you have fastened off your yarn, you will need to hide the ends of the yarn by weaving them into the rows. If you skip this step and simply cut them off, you will always have a knot with a bit of frayed yarn showing.

Thread a plastic yarn needle onto the end of the yarn. Weave the yarn into the crocheted row by stitching in and out with the needle a few times (about 3 to 4 stitches). Cut off the extra yarn.

SEWING PIECES TOGETHER WITH A WHIP STITCH

Sometimes a project is made by crocheting a few pieces and then sewing them together. If you leave a long tail of yarn when you finish crocheting, you can use the tail to sew with. If you don't have a long tail of yarn, you can tie a new piece of yarn to one of the corners of the piece.

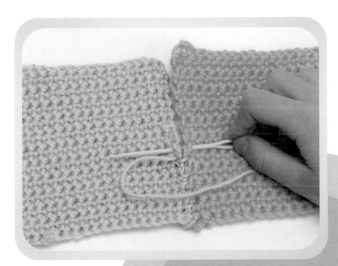

Lay the pieces flat with the seams close together. Start with the yarn attached to the corner of one piece. Thread a yarn needle onto the yarn. Stitch the two pieces together as shown, sewing through both sections. Pull the yarn tight. Bring the yarn up and over again for the next stitch a little bit away from the last stitch. Continue to stitch up the seam. At the end of the seam, tie the end of the yarn to one side with a knot. Hide the end of the yarn by weaving it into the crocheted rows. Cut off the extra yarn.

stuff to make!

n ow comes the fun part—using all the great skills you just learned to make cool crochet projects for yourself and your friends. There's jewelry, purses, belts, and pillows to decorate your room—even a few special things to surprise your favorite pets. So grab your yarn and hook, and read on!

best-friend bracelets

make a few of these colorful bracelets for yourself and your BFF! You can use any type of yarn, including fancy yarn and ribbon. This "tie on" bracelet can be left on until it wears out or until you are ready to replace it with a new one.

- Yarn or ribbon yarn scraps (at least 1 yard per bracelet)
- Size G (6) or H (8) crochet hook, depending on the weight of the yarn
- Scissors

1 Follow the instructions on page 19 to make a slipknot, leaving a 6-inch tail. (The tail will be used later to tie the bracelet onto your wrist.) Then make a foundation chain. Keep making chain stitches until the bracelet fits around your wrist.

2 To finish, cut off the yarn about 6 inches from the last stitch. Use your crochet hook to pull the yarn all the way through the last stitch.

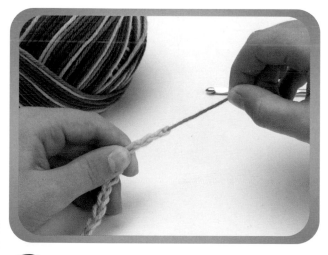

3 Pull the end of the yarn tightly to finish.

4 Tie the ends of the yarn in a knot around your wrist. Use your fingers as shown to hold the yarn as you tighten the knot, or have a friend help you.

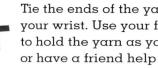

ribbon shoelaces

make your sneaks a fashion statement with a pair of personalized shoelaces! Ribbon yarn is good to use for shoelaces because it's smooth and easier to thread through shoelace loops than regular yarn. Plus, it comes in a variety of bright colors and textures.

materials

* Ribbon yarn (at least 1 ball per lace)
* Size G (6) crochet hook
* Scissors
* White glue or Fray Check

1 Follow the directions on pages 19 and 21 to make a slipknot and a chain stitch. Continue making chain stitches until the chain is as long as your shoelaces. (Hint: Use the laces from your shoes as a guide for how long to make the chain. Shoelaces are usually 36 inches or longer.)

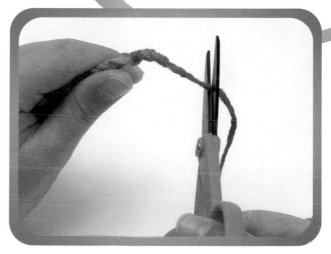

2 After the chain is as long as a shoelace, cut off the yarn about 6 inches from the last stitch. Pull the end of the yarn through the last stitch and pull tight. Clip the yarn off on both ends, about 1½ inches from the last stitch. Follow steps 1 and 2 to make another lace to match the first.

3 Coat the ends of the crocheted shoelaces with glue or Fray Check, covering about 1 inch of each end. Let the glue dry. This will stiffen the ends, making them easier to lace up. (Hint: Wax paper is a perfect surface for drying the glued ends, as you can peel them off easily when the glue is dry. Or hang the shoelaces over a towel rack to dry.)

button-up bracelet

this bracelet is similar to the Best-Friend Bracelets on page 32, but has a button and loop closure so you can take it on and off.

* Yarn or ribbon yarn scraps (at least 1 yard per bracelet)
* Size G (6) or H (8) crochet hook, depending on the weight of the yarn
* Button (with shank on back—this is a loop used to sew the button to fabric)
* Scissors
* White glue or Fray Check (optional)

1 Thread the yarn through the shank and slide the button onto the yarn.

2 Make a slipknot about 6 inches from the end of the yarn. Slide the button toward the ball of yarn to keep it out of the way as you make the knot. Insert the hook into the slipknot loop.

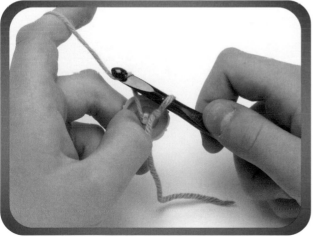

3 Slide the button back up to the knot. Hook the yarn over and pull the yarn through the loop on the hook to make one chain stitch. The button will be attached by the first stitch.

4 Continue making chain stitches until the bracelet fits around your wrist.

continued on next page 37

5 Cut off the string about 12 inches from the last stitch. Bring the end of the string through the last stitch loop. Don't pull tight—this will be the loop you slide over the button.

6 Measure the loop by holding it next to the button and making sure the loop will pass over the button. Adjust the size of the loop by pulling the end of the yarn.

7 Tie the end of the yarn around the base of the loop a few times, making a knot to hold the loop in place. Weave the yarn ends back through the chain for a few stitches on each end to hide. Clip off the extra yarn. For extra security, put a drop of glue over the knot on the loop end of the bracelet. Let the glue dry before wearing the bracelet.

bead-dazzled rings

these rings are made from elastic thread, so they're extra stretchy and will fit perfectly on your fingers. Elastic thread comes in different colors, including gold and silver. Why not make a ring to match each of your favorite outfits? This ring uses three beads, but you can use one, two, or more if you want.

materials

* Elastic thread (at least 1 roll per ring)
* Size F (5) crochet hook or smaller
* Small beads with holes big enough for elastic thread
* Scissors
* White glue or Fray Check

1 Thread the beads onto the elastic before beginning to crochet. Then slide the beads down the elastic, out of the way. Leave about a 3-inch tail at the end of the elastic and make a slipknot. Insert the hook and begin to crochet chain stitches (see page 21), occasionally stopping to measure the chain around your finger.

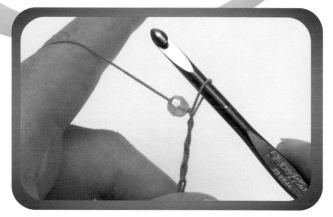

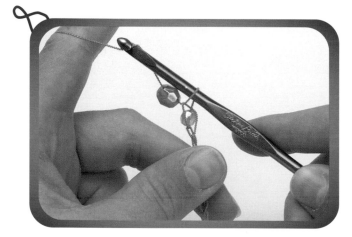

2 When the chain fits around *half* of your finger snugly, slide a bead close to the loop on the hook.

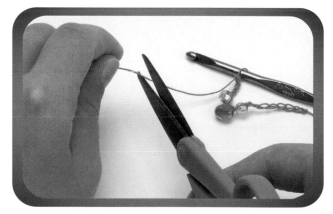

3 Hook the elastic *after* the bead and pull the elastic through the loop on the hook to make a chain stitch, holding the bead in place. Slide up the next bead and do the same thing, hooking the elastic *after* the bead. Do the same with a third bead. Then continue to crochet chain stitches until the chain fits all of the way around your finger.

4 Cut the end of the elastic about 3 inches from the last stitch. Hook the elastic through the loop on the hook and pull to finish.

5 Tie the ends in a knot, pulling tightly.

6 Clip off the ends close to the knot. Put a dot of white glue on the knot and let it dry.

princess necklace

This pattern uses cotton thread and beads to make an easy, pretty necklace. Make it as long or short as you want. Add a bead every few inches, or add groups of beads on more stitches for a different look. Play around to create your own, one-of-a-kind look!

materials

* 1 ball of crochet thread (cotton or cotton blend)
* Size G (6) crochet hook or smaller
* 17 beads with holes large enough for the thread to pass through
* Small piece of craft wire (about 4 inches)
* Scissors

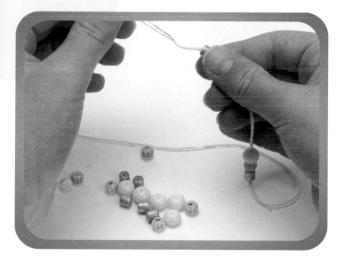

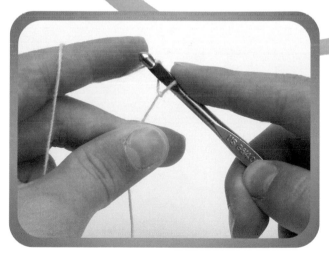

1 Thread all 17 beads onto the string before you begin to crochet. To help string the beads, make a "beading needle" out of wire: Take a small piece of craft wire and bend it in half, catching the cotton thread in the bend of the wire. Then pass the wire beading needle through the holes in the beads.

2 Slide the beads down the thread and out of the way. Leaving an 8-inch tail at the end of the thread, make a slipknot and insert the hook. Bring the yarn over the hook and make about 10 chain stitches (see page 21).

continued on next page

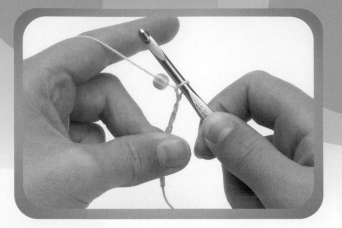 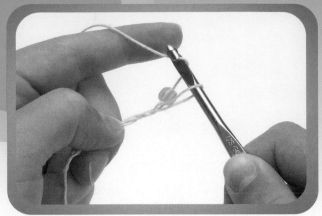

3 To add a bead, slide the first bead up, close to the stitching.

4 Hook the yarn over, making a stitch *after* the bead. Pull the thread through the loop on the hook. Then make 4 regular chain stitches.

44

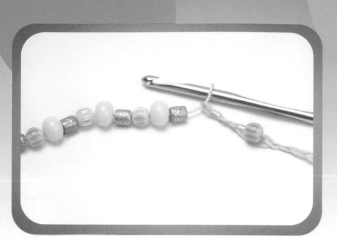

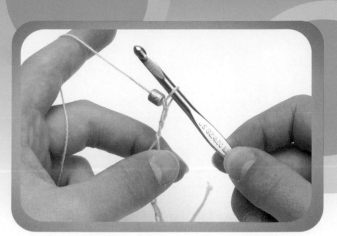

5 This photo shows one bead crocheted into the chain. The rest of the beads are strung and ready to be added one at a time as you crochet.

6 Repeat steps 3–4 to add another bead. Continue in this manner, adding each bead in turn and then crocheting 4 chain stitches, until the necklace reaches the desired length.

7 To finish, cut off the end of the string 6 inches from the last stitch and pull the string through the last chain stitch. Use the ends of the string to tie the necklace around your neck.

"The more you dress up, the more fun you'll have."

—Brian Molko

JOINING NEW YARN

Okay, so you're crocheting and suddenly you run out of yarn! What then? No problem. Simply join on a new ball of yarn. Whenever possible, join yarn at the end of a row. Simply tie the new yarn around the old, leaving a 6-inch tail. After you have crocheted a few rows, untie the knot and weave in the yarn ends.

hip-tie belt

jute is a type of string that is commonly used for macramé, but it is also easy to crochet with. Combine different colors of jute and beads to make cool crochet belts to match all of your favorite tops. Be sure to crochet the belt loosely for a casual look.

- 1 ball of colored jute string
- 17 plastic pony beads or other beads (make sure the holes are large enough for the string to pass through)
- Size G (6) crochet hook
- Scissors

1 Thread all 17 beads onto the string before you begin to crochet. Slide the beads down toward the ball of jute to keep them out of the way.

2 Make a slipknot, leaving an 8-inch tail at the end of the string (this will be used later for the fringe). Crochet a row of chain stitches (see page 21) until the belt is long enough to fit around your waist with about 6 inches extra for tying.

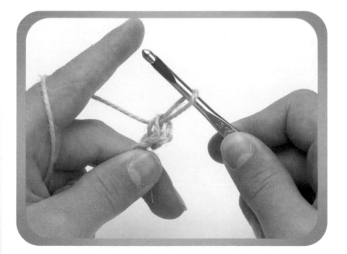

3 Now you're going to start a row of single crochet stitches. Insert the hook into the second stitch from the hook and crochet 8 single crochet stitches (see pages 22–25).

4 To add your first bead, slide the top bead up from the beads already threaded on the ball of string.

continued on next page

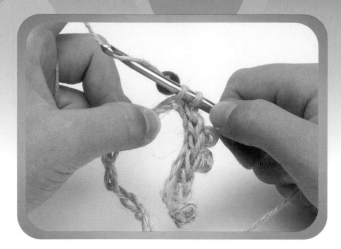

5 Slide the bead close to the stitching, then insert the hook into the next chain stitch. Hook the string over, *after* the bead and pull the string through the *first* loop on the hook to crochet the bead in place.

6 Hook the string over again and pull the string through *both* loops to complete the stitch.

7 This photo shows the completed single crochet stitch from behind the bead. Make 5 single crochet stitches and then repeat steps 4–6 to add another bead. Continue in this manner: adding a bead, doing 5 single crochet stitches, adding another bead, and so on.

    As you get close to the end, stop adding beads and single crochet to the end of the belt. Make a single chain stitch at the end of the row. Cut off the string about 8 inches from the last stitch and pull the end through the chain stitch to finish.

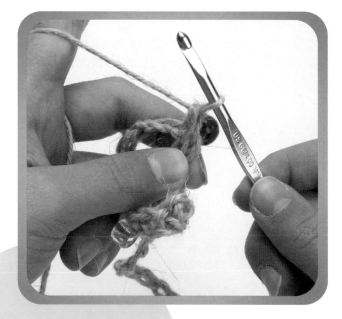

8 Now make the fringe. Notice how the end you just finished has two 8-inch strings hanging from it. Cut another piece of string about 16 inches long. Fold this string in half and push the folded end through one of the stitches at the end of the belt, forming a loop.

9 Pull the ends of the string through the loop and pull tight. This will give you 4 strands for the fringe. Cut two more 16-inch-long pieces of string. Repeat steps 8–9 to attach these pieces to the other end of the belt. Tie beads on the ends of the fringe for added decoration.

pamper-your-pooch pet blanket

bulky, thick yarns let you crochet projects super quick. This yarn is very soft—perfect for making fluffy bed blankets for all your favorite pets!

materials

- 1 skein Lion Brand Big Yarn
- Jumbo size Q crochet hook
- Scissors

1 Make a slipknot near the end of the yarn and chain 15 stitches (see page 21). Then start your first row. Insert the hook into the second stitch from the hook and make single crochet stitches along the row (see pages 22–25). You should end up with 14 stitches. At the end of the row, make a single chain stitch.

2 Turn the work over and do another row, making 14 single crochet stitches. Make a single chain stitch at the end of the row. Turn the work over to begin the next row. Continue in this manner, making 14 single crochet stitches plus one chain stitch at the end of each row until you have completed about 14 rows.

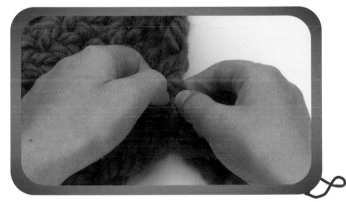

3 You will probably run out of yarn by the time you reach row 14. If your yarn is running short, stop at rows 12 or 13. Pull the end of the yarn through the last stitch at the end of the row to finish. Pull tight.

4 Weave the end of the yarn through the last row with your fingers or a hook.

5 Cut off the extra yarn.

purrrr-fect cat toys

Cats love yarn and small toys. If you want, you can even add a bit of catnip to the stuffing before sewing up the toy. Just be sure to use cotton or acrylic yarn, because wool fibers are dangerous for cats to swallow.

1 Make a slipknot close to the end of the yarn. Insert the hook and crochet 8 chain stitches (see page 21). To start the first row, insert the hook into the second stitch from the hook and crochet 7 single crochet stitches (see pages 22–25), one for each chain stitch. Make a single chain stitch at the end of the row.

2 Turn the work over and begin the next row, making 7 single crochet stitches across. Make a single chain stitch at the end of the row. Continue crocheting rows like this until you have about 14 rows. The finished piece should form a square when you fold it in half. Finish the last row by cutting the yarn about 3 inches away from the last stitch. Pull the end of the yarn through the last stitch at the end of the row and pull to tighten.

4 Use a yarn needle and a long piece of yarn to whip stitch (see page 29) two of the sides shut. Leave the needle and yarn attached. You'll leave the third side open so you can put in the stuffing.

3 Fold the crocheted rectangle in half to make a square.

5 Stuff the toy with polyfill or batting and a bell—if you want noise. Then use the yarn needle and attached yarn to sew the last side shut. Tie the yarn in a knot and cut off the extra yarn.

stretchy headband

Use a solid-colored yarn to match your clothes, or have fun with a novelty yarn that will add sparkle to your hair! Elastic is used in this project to make sure the headband fits perfectly around your head.

1 Make a slipknot close to the end of the yarn and crochet 7 chain stitches (see page 21). To start the first row, insert the hook into the second stitch from the hook and do 6 single crochet stitches, (see pages 22–25) one for each chain stitch. Make a single chain stitch at the end of the row.

2 Turn the work over and begin the next row, making 6 single crochet stitches across. Make a single chain stitch at the end of the row. Continue crocheting rows until you have about 75 short rows, or until it almost fits around your head. Measure the band around your head and crochet until it's a few inches short of fitting around your head (you want to leave a few inches for the elastic).

3 Cut the end of the yarn about 6 inches from the last stitch. Pull the end of the yarn through the last stitch at the end of the row. Use a yarn needle to weave the yarn through the stitching to hide the end of the yarn. Clip off any extra yarn.

continued on next page 55

4 Thread a sewing needle with a thread. Pull the thread long enough to have a doubled piece of thread for strength. Knot the end of the thread and sew one end of the elastic to the end of the crocheted headband. Bring the needle through the yarn and then through the elastic.

5 Whip stitch (see page 29) along the edge of the elastic, sewing it to the headband. Tie a knot in the end of the thread and clip off the extra to finish. Measure the band with the elastic around your head. Use your thumb to mark how tight to sew the elastic to the other side.

6 Cut off the extra elastic and sew the end of the elastic to the other side of the headband to finish.

BE EARTH-FRIENDLY!

When you are finished with a crochet project, don't throw away the extra yarn! Use your yarn remnants to make matching accessories, like rings, bracelets, or even shoelaces.

bathing beauty bath mitt

this bath mitt *is* made of cotton yarn, which means you can get it wet and soapy, just like any washcloth! You can make the mitt to fit your hand (which might be smaller than the pattern calls for). Simply crochet a row of stitches that *is* as wide as your hand, and then crochet rows until the rectangle folds in half over the top of your hand.

materials

* 1 ball (or skein) cotton yarn
* Crochet hook size G
* Yarn needle
* Scissors

1 Make a slipknot and 25 chain stitches (see page 21), or however many you need to fit across the width of your hand. Begin the first row of single crochet stitches (see pages 22–25) by hooking into the second chain stitch from the hook. Then work 24 single crochet stitches in the row. Make a chain stitch at the end of the row and turn the work to start the next row.

2 Start the second row by inserting the hook into the first single crochet stitch from the hook. Keep crocheting rows; remember to add the single chain stitch at the end of each row. Count the stitches to make sure you always have 24 in the row plus the extra chain stitch at the end of the row. Crochet about 60 rows until you have a long rectangle that can be folded in half to fit over your hand.

Fold

3 Leave the loop in the last chain stitch; don't cut the yarn or tie a knot. Remove the hook and fold the rectangle in half. Bring the first row to match up with the last row as you fold the rectangle.

continued on next page

"When all else fails, take a bath."

—Rita Sherman

Start Here

4 Start at the corner and insert the hook through both layers. Then make a single crochet stitch to connect the sides.

5 Keep crocheting across the fold (even though you aren't closing a side). This will allow you to reach the other side without having to cut the yarn. It also makes a nice-looking edge across the top of the mitt. Continue crocheting the remaining side shut, inserting the hook through both layers and making single crochet stitches along the edges.

6 When you reach the corner of the mitt, cut the yarn, leaving a 6-inch tail. Pull the tail through the last stitch to finish off. Pull the yarn tight and use a yarn needle to weave the tails of yarn back through the edges to hide. Cut off the extra yarn.

keepsake coin purse

this purse is just the right size for holding money, lip balm, or your keys—and you can slip it right in your pocket or backpack! Choose a favorite button to keep the purse closed.

- 1 ball of heavy cotton yarn
- Size H (8) crochet hook
- Button
- Yarn needle
- Sewing needle
- Sewing thread and thread

1 Make a slipknot close to the end of the yarn and crochet 12 chain stitches (see page 21). To start the first row, insert the hook into the second stitch from the hook and crochet 11 single crochet stitches (see pages 22–25), one for each chain stitch. Make a single chain stitch at the end of the row. This completes one row.

2 Turn the work over and begin the next row, doing 11 single crochet stitches across. Make a chain stitch at the end of the row. Continue crocheting rows until you have about 26 rows. To see if it's big enough, fold the bottom up to form the purse, leaving enough rows for a flap. Crochet a few more rows if needed.

3 When it's big enough, crochet this last row to form a button loop. Starting at the beginning of the row, make 4 single crochet stitches. Then crochet 5 chain stitches—these will not be connected to the row.

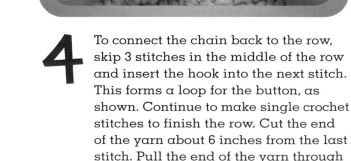

4 To connect the chain back to the row, skip 3 stitches in the middle of the row and insert the hook into the next stitch. This forms a loop for the button, as shown. Continue to make single crochet stitches to finish the row. Cut the end of the yarn about 6 inches from the last stitch. Pull the end of the yarn through the last chain stitch at the end of the row to finish off.

5 Fold the bottom up to form the purse.

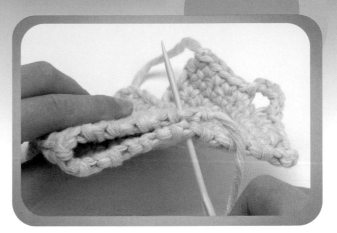

6 Cut a piece of yarn about 24 inches long and thread a yarn needle. Tie the yarn to one of the corners and sew up the side using a whip stitch (see page 29). Repeat on the other side, tying a knot to finish. Weave the ends of the yarn inside the stitching of the purse to hide.

7 Use a sewing needle and thread to sew a button to the front of the purse.

"A penny saved is a penny earned."

—Ben Franklin

cuddly scarf

textured yarns are a little tricky to crochet with because it can be hard to see the stitches in the texture. So you may want to make a few projects with solid yarn before starting this one. The nice thing about textured yarn is that it feels so soft. And if you do miss a stitch, no problem! The yarn hides your mistakes!

materials

* 1 skein of textured yarn
* Size P (16) crochet hook
* Yarn needle
* Scissors

SCARF SMARTS

One way to figure out scarf length is to hold your arms straight out from your sides and measure the distance from fingertip to fingertip. Stop crocheting when the chain reaches all the way across while you are holding your arms out.

1 Make a slipknot about 6 inches from the end of the yarn. Then make a row of chain stitches that's as long as you want your scarf to be (see page 21).

2 To start your first row, insert the hook into the second chain stitch from the hook and begin to crochet, making one single crochet stitch (see pages 22–25) in each chain stitch. Keep the row of chain stitches facing the same way as you crochet—if it gets twisted it's hard to see which chain to crochet into. Make a single chain stitch at the end of the row. This completes one row.

continued on next page

3 Turn the work over and begin the next row, making single crochet stitches across the row and a single chain stitch at the end of the row. Continue crocheting rows until you have about 7 long rows, or until it's as wide as you would like.

4 At the end of the last row, cut off the end of the yarn about 6 inches from the last stitch. Pull the end through the last single crochet stitch and pull to finish off. Use a yarn needle to weave the ends of the yarn into the rows to hide.

5 Now make fringe tassels for the ends. First, cut 18 pieces of yarn, each 18 inches long. Divide them into groups of three. Take one group of three strands and fold in half. Pull the middle of the strands through one of the corners of the scarf with the hook.

6 Pull the strands through to make a loop.

> "A friend is one of the nicest things you can have, and one of the best things you can be."
>
> —Douglas Pagels

7 Pull the ends of the strands through the loop and pull tightly. Repeat steps 5–6 to add a tassel to the middle and one to the other corner. Then create the same three fringe tassels at the other end of the scarf. Trim the ends of the fringe to make them even.

striped scarf

Choose your three favorite colors to make this bold, colorful scarf! This pattern will show you how to change colors as you crochet, so you can create stripes and other patterns.

- 3 skeins of worsted-weight yarn (1 for each color)
- Size H (8) crochet hook
- Yarn needle
- Scissors

1 Start with one of your three colors. Follow steps 1–3 for the Cuddly Scarf on pages 65–66, but stop before doing the last stitch on the second row. A new color will be added to this stitch.

2 Insert the hook to begin the last stitch in the row. Hook the yarn over and pull the yarn through the stitch, so that you have two loops on the hook (just as you would for the first half of a single crochet stitch). Stop here and add the new color. Instead of pulling the yarn through both loops to finish the stitch, you will add the new color to pull through instead.

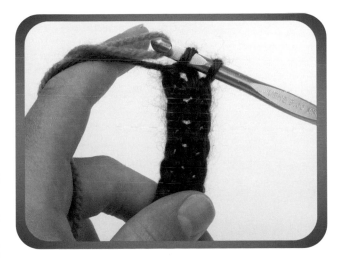

3 Hook the new color yarn, leaving a 6-inch tail on the end of the new yarn.

4 Pull the new yarn through both loops on the hook. Now you have one loop of the new color on the hook.

continued on next page

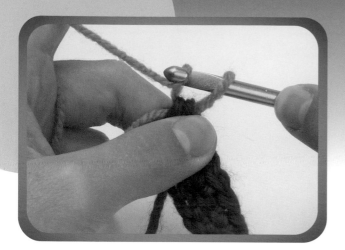

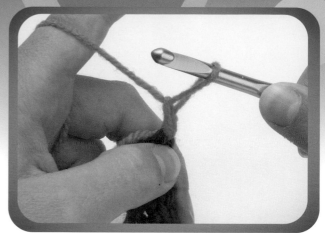

5 Make the chain stitch at the end of the row with the new yarn (hook the yarn over and pull it through the loop on the hook).

6 This photo shows the finished chain stitch on the end of the row with the new yarn. Cut off the first color, leaving a tail about 6 inches long. You can weave this into the scarf later.

7 Turn the work over to start a new row. Insert the hook into the first stitch in the row and do a single crochet stitch. Continue doing single crochet stitches down the row. Add the single chain stitch at the end of the row and turn the work over to complete another row. Stop before doing the last stitch.

8 Repeat steps 2–7 to add the *third* color yarn.

way to crochet!

9 Continue in this manner, crocheting two rows of each color until you have 14 rows. The first two rows should be the same color as the last two rows. When you're done, cut the end of the yarn and pull through the last stitch to finish off. Pull tightly and weave the end of the yarn through the rows with a yarn needle. Weave the other ends between the rows in the same fashion. Cut off the extra yarn.

10 Now make five tassels to decorate each end. Cut 20 pieces of yarn, each about 12 inches long. Divide the pieces into groups of four. Fold the first group of four strands in half.

11 Use a hook to pull the yarn group through one of the corners of the scarf.

12 Pull the yarn through the scarf to form a loop.

continued on next page

13 Bring the ends of the yarn through the loop.

14 Pull tightly to finish. Add the other four groups along the edge. Then repeat for the other end. Trim the ends of the fringe tassels to make them even.

COLOR YOUR WORLD!

arns come in all sorts of beautiful colors. When combining colors, be bold! Put skeins and balls of your favorite colors together to see what combinations you like best. You can choose different shades of the same color, such as light, medium, and dark blue, or combine opposites, like yellow and purple, or red and green, for a more lively look. It's also a good idea to check yarn colors against whatever jacket, coat, or sweaters you wear most often to see what makes a good match. Check out page 109 to learn more about matching colors.

rainbow yarn purse

Purses are super-quick to make—they're just a rectangle sewn in half with an opening at the top! The strap is made by crocheting a row of single crochet stitches. This one is crocheted in chunky, soft, colorful yarn that makes a great bag for yourself, or a gift for a friend.

materials

- 1 skein of Jiffy Thick & Quick yarn (Lion Brand)
- Size P (16) crochet hook
- Yarn needle

1 Make a slipknot close to the end of the yarn and crochet 17 chain stitches (see page 21). To make your first row, insert the hook into the second stitch from the hook and make 16 single crochet stitches (see pages 22–25), one for each chain stitch. Make a single chain stitch at the end of the row.

2 Turn the work over and begin the next row, making 16 single crochet stitches across. Make a chain stitch at the end of the row. Continue crocheting rows until you have about 28 rows. Don't forget the chain stitch at the end of each row!

3 At the end of the last row, cut off the yarn about 3 inches from the last stitch. Pull the end through the last single crochet stitch and pull to finish. Use a yarn needle to weave the ends of the yarn into the rows to hide.

4 Fold the rectangle you have just crocheted in half to form the purse. Cut a piece of yarn about 24 inches long and thread it onto the yarn needle. Tie the piece to the inside of the purse in the corner fold on one side. Use the needle to whip stitch (see page 29) the side of the purse closed. Tie a knot to finish. Cut the end of the yarn, leaving a 3-inch tail. Weave the ends into the purse to hide. Tuck the knot inside he purse. Repeat to stitch up the other side of the purse.

continued on next page

5 Now make the strap. Tie the end of your ball of yarn to one side of the purse. Insert the hook into the purse and pull a loop of thread up to begin a chain stitch. Wrap the yarn over the hook to make a chain stitch.

6 Continue making a chain stitch until you have chained 44 stitches.

7 Without removing the hook, insert the hook into the other side of the purse.

8 Wrap the yarn over the hook and pull a loop through the purse and through the loop on the hook.

> "A best friend is like a four-leaf clover,
> hard to find and lucky to have."
>
> —Anonymous

TAKE A BREAK!

When you take a crochet break, add a paper clip to your last stitch. This way, when you pick up your project after your break, you'll know exactly where you left off—and you won't mess up the project!

9 To make the strap extra sturdy, insert the hook into the next stitch. For a thicker strap, crochet a row of single crochet stitches along the chain. This will widen the strap. Crochet until you reach the other side.

10 At the end of the row, cut off the end of the yarn about 6 inches from the last stitch. Pull the end through the last single crochet stitch and pull to finish. Use a yarn needle to weave the ends of the yarn into the sides of the purse to hide.

sunny fabric purse

this purse is made by crocheting strips of fabric! When you hunt for fabric, pick one with a background color you like. Don't worry about the pattern—you won't be able to see it anyway. You can mix different fabric strips if you want multicolored stripes in your purse.

materials

* 2 yards cotton fabric
* Scissors
* Size P (16) crochet hook
* Yarn needle

1 To tear the fabric into ³/₄-inch strips, start by making a small clip with scissors. Then tear about 10 strips with the grain (this is the long way on the fabric).

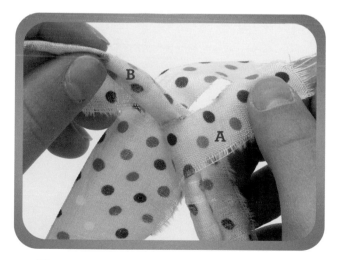

2 Fold the end of each strip over about 1 inch and cut a small slit (be careful not to cut through the end of the strip).

3 Slip the end of strip B through the slit in strip A, as shown above.

continued on next page

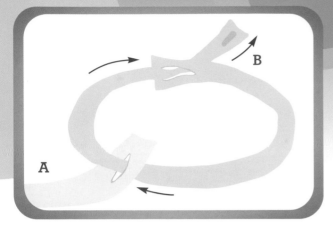

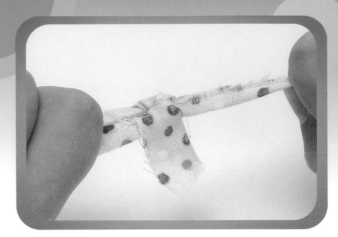

4 Bring the tail of strip B back through its own slit at the other end.

5 Pull the strips gently until they are tight. Then join the remaining nine strips into one long strip.

6 When all the strips are joined, wind them into a ball to crochet with. You can add additional strips as needed while you are crocheting.

7 Now start as usual, using the fabric strips as yarn. Make a slipknot close to the end of the fabric strip. Insert the hook and crochet 13 chain stitches (see page 21). To start the first row, insert the hook into the second stitch from the hook and make 12 single crochet stitches (see pages 22–25), one for each chain stitch. Make a single chain stitch at the end of the row.

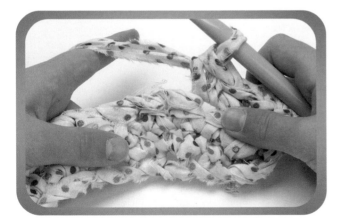

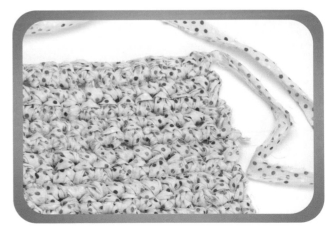

8 Turn the work over and begin the next row, doing 12 single crochet stitches across. Make a chain stitch at the end of the row. Continue crocheting rows until you have about 21 rows (remember the chain stitch at the end of each row). If you run out of yarn, just add more fabric strips, connecting them with the slit method.

9 At the end of the last row, pull the end of the last strip through the last single crochet stitch and pull to finish off. Leave this tail to sew up the side.

10 Fold the rectangle you have just crocheted in half to form the purse.

12 To close the other side of the purse, tie another strip of fabric to the top corner of that side and use it to whip stitch (see page 29) the opening closed. Tie a knot and hide it inside the purse.

11 Thread a yarn needle onto the end of the fabric tail and sew that side closed with a whip stitch (see page 29). Add more strips if needed as you sew. Tie a knot at the bottom corner of the purse, hiding the knot inside the purse. Clip off any extra fabric and weave into the purse to hide.

"Some people weave burlap into the fabric of our lives, and some weave gold thread. Both contribute to make the whole picture beautiful and unique."

—*Anonymous*

13 Now make the strap. Tie the end of a new strip of fabric to one side of the purse.

continued on next page

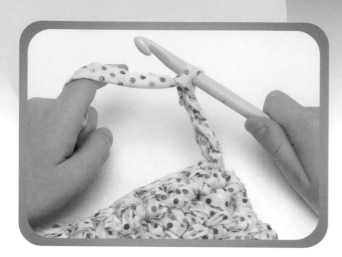

15 To attach the strap, follow steps 7–8 for the Rainbow Yarn Purse on page 76.

14 Insert the hook into the purse and pull a loop of fabric up to begin a chain stitch. Wrap the fabric strip over the hook to make a stitch. Continue making a chain stitch until you have chained 50 stitches.

16 To make the strap extra sturdy, take the tail end of the strip and tie it again to the inside of the purse, making a knot. Clip off the end and weave it inside the purse through the stitches to hide.

save-the-planet
purselet

Want to be earth-friendly? Recycle plastic bags by turning them into a cute purse! Best of all, it won't cost you cent. The crocheted plastic is surprisingly strong and has a nice feel to it.

materials

* 10 plastic grocery bags or 5 large plastic garbage bags
* 1 Scissors
* 1 Size P (16) crochet hook
* 1 Yarn needle

1 Smooth and flatten the bags. Stack five at a time and fold the stack in half lengthwise. Cut the bags into 1-inch strips across the width of the bags.

2 Join the strips by looping them together. (These photos use two colors so you can easily see how to join them. For a solid-colored purse, you would be joining the same color loops.) Loop the blue loop through the red loop.

continued on next page

"One thing you can't recycle is wasted time."

—*Author Unknown*

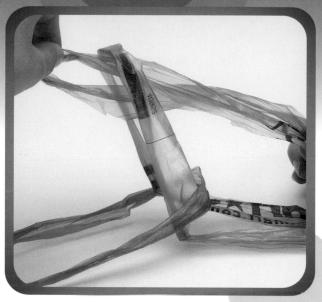

3 Pull the end of the blue loop back through itself.

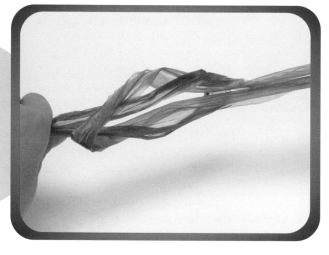

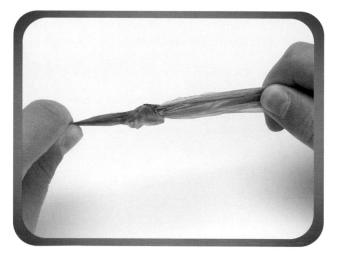

4 Pull the loops gently until they are tight, but not too tight or they will tear.

5 Add another loop to the end of the two you just joined, following steps 2–4. Keep adding plastic loops until you have joined all of the strips. Wind the strips into a ball.

SEEING DOUBLE

The connected loops give you a double strand of "yarn," but when you crochet treat them as one strand, keeping the strands together.

6 Now crochet as usual, using the joined plastic loops as "yarn." Make a slipknot close at the end of the "yarn." Insert the hook and crochet 13 chain stitches (*see* page 21). To start the first row, insert the hook into the second stitch from the hook and do 12 single crochet stitches (*see* pages 22–25), one for each chain stitch. Make a single chain stitch at the end of the row.

7 Turn the work over and begin the next row, doing 12 single crochet stitches across. Make a chain stitch at the end of the row. Continue crocheting rows until you have about 19 rows, remembering the chain stitch at the end of each row. If you run out of "yarn," just add more plastic loops.

8 At the end of the last row, pull the end of the last loop through the last single crochet stitch and pull to finish off. Leave this tail to sew up the side.

continued on next page

9 Fold the rectangle you have just crocheted in half to form the purse. Thread a yarn needle onto the plastic tail and sew the side closed with a whip stitch (see page 29). Add more loops if needed as you sew.

10 Tie a knot at the bottom corner of the purse, hiding the knot inside of the purse. Clip off any extra plastic and weave into the purse to hide. Use the needle to whip stitch the side of the purse closed. Tie another loop of plastic to the top corner of the other side and stitch that side up, too. Tie a knot and hide it inside the purse.

11 To make a different-colored border around the top of the purse, attach a loop of different-colored plastic through one of the stitches on one side at the top of the purse. Pull the end through itself just as you did to connect loops. Pull tight. Add more loops of plastic to the end of this one to give you enough to crochet around the top.

12 Single crochet around the top of the purse with the new color, inserting the hook into the top of the purse for each stitch.

13 After you have crocheted all the way around the top, connect more strips to make the strap. Start crocheting the strap using a chain stitch. Crochet about 44 chain stitches to form the strap.

14 Insert the hook into the other side of the purse and wrap the plastic over the hook. Pull a loop through the purse and through the loop on the hook. Wrap the end of the plastic over the hook again and pull completely through the loop to finish off, pulling tightly. Take the tail end of the loop and tie it again to the inside of one of the stitches inside the purse, making a knot. Clip off the extra and weave it through the stitches inside the purse to hide.

"There are big ships and small ships. But the best ship of all is friendship."

—Author Unknown

itty-bitty backpack

Who doesn't need this cute backpack, just the right size for your favorite book and a few essentials? We used a bulky yarn, which makes it extra-quick to make. Add a splash of color with a ribbon and beads to keep it closed.

materials

- 1 skein of Lion Brand Big Yarn
- Jumbo size Q crochet hook
- Scissors
- 1 yard of ribbon
- 2 large wooden beads
- White glue or fabric glue

1 Make a slipknot near the end of the yarn and make 9 chain stitches (see page 21). To start your first row, insert the hook into the second stitch from the hook and make 8 single crochet stitches (see pages 22–25), one for each chain stitch. Make a single chain stitch at the end of the row.

2 Turn the work over and begin the next row, making 8 single crochet stitches across. Make a chain stitch at the end of the row. Continue crocheting rows until you have about 21 rows. Don't forget the chain stitch at the end of each row.

3 Cut the end of the yarn about 24 inches from the last stitch. Pull the end of the yarn through the stitch at the end of the row to finish and pull tight.

4 Fold the crocheted piece in half to form the backpack.

continued on next page

5 Use the 24-inch long yarn tail from step 3 to sew one side closed. Use your hook to pull the yarn through both layers of the backpack. Bring the yarn over, forming a whip stitch (see page 29) and continuing down the side to stitch it closed using the hook instead of a needle. Tie a knot at the bottom corner and hide the knot inside the backpack. Trim off the extra yarn and weave into the stitching to hide.

6 Tie another 24 inch piece of yarn to a corner on the other side, and repeat step 5 to sew the other side closed.

7 Now make the straps. Tie the yarn to the top corner on the inside of the backpack. Insert the hook through a nearby stitch and pull the yarn through to make a loop.

8 Use this loop to start a row of chain stitches for the strap. Make about 30 chain stitches for the strap.

"Don't forget to pack your courage
for your journey to greatness."

—David Weinbaum

 Hook into the bottom corner and hook the yarn over, pulling the yarn all the way through the backpack and the loop on the hook. Cut off the yarn, leaving enough to tie a knot. Tie a knot and weave the yarn end into the inside of the backpack. Repeat steps 7–9 to make a strap for the other side.

10 To make a tie to close the backpack, cut a piece of ribbon about 24 inches long. Weave the ribbon through the front of the backpack about 2 inches from the side and then through the back, using your hook to help if necessary. Run the ribbon back out to the front as shown. Pull the ends to make them even on the front of the backpack.

continued on next page

11 Finish by sliding a large wooden bead on each end of the ribbon. Tie a big knot to hold the bead in place (tie several knots on top of each other if necessary to make a bigger knot). Use a little white glue on the cut ends of the ribbon to prevent fraying. Let the glue dry.

MAKE A FASHION STATEMENT!

Personalize your backpack or purse with funky pins, key chains, or patches. It's easy to attach these items to the yarn either by sewing them on or using fabric glue.

"The only way to have a
friend is to be one."

—Ralph Waldo Emerson

pom-pom pillow

Choose your favorite colors for this fun, cheery pillow. This project teaches you how to sew crocheted squares together. You can make striped pillows, rectangle shapes, or solid-colored pillows for a different look. Pom-poms add a little extra decoration for the corners.

* 4 skeins worsted weight yarn in different colors
* Size I (9) crochet hook
* Scissors
* Yarn needle
* Polyfill stuffing
* Ruler

1 You're going to crochet four squares, each a different color. Start with your first color. Make a slipknot near the end of the yarn and 21 chain stitches (see page 21). To start your first row, insert the hook into the second stitch from the hook and make 20 single crochet stitches (see pages 22–25), one for each chain stitch. Make a single chain stitch at the end of the row.

2 Turn the work over and begin the next row, making 20 single crochet stitches across. Make a chain stitch at the end of the row. Continue crocheting rows until you have a square (about 20–22 rows). When you have finished the square, cut the end of the yarn about 6 inches from the last stitch. Pull the end of the yarn through the last stitch at the end of the row to finish and pull tight.

continued on next page

SQUARE IT UP

An easy way to see if your piece is a perfect square is to fold it diagonally. The sides will be even if it's square.

"Wear cute pajamas, you'll never know who you'll meet in your dreams."

— *Author Unknown*

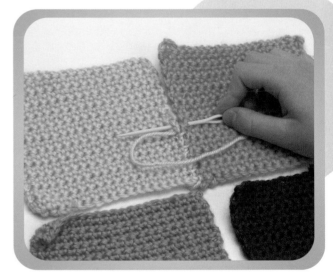

3 Make three more squares in different colors following steps 1–2. Don't worry if they aren't all perfectly the same.

4 Sew two squares together with the color of yarn from one of the squares. Thread a yarn needle with a few feet of yarn and tie the yarn to the corner of one of the squares. Whip stitch (see page 29) the two squares together. If one square is a little bigger than the other, stretch it to fit the other square as you sew. After sewing the squares together, tie a knot on the back of the seam. Clip off the yarn and weave the yarn into the crocheted rows to hide.

5 Repeat step 4 to sew the other two squares together. Then sew both pairs together to complete the front of the pillow.

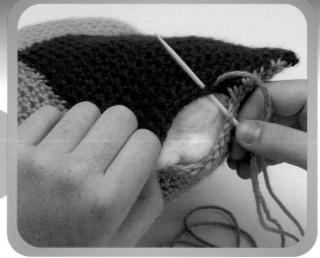

6 To make the back of the pillow, choose one of the colors and crochet a large square. Make a slipknot and crochet 41 chain stitches. Then do rows of 40 single crochet stitches, with a chain stitch at the end of each row. Crochet until you have a square (about 40–42 rows). Finish by cutting off the yarn and pulling the tail through the last chain stitch.

7 Sew the front of the pillow to the back using a long piece of yarn. Tie the yarn to the corner of the back piece and sew the sides together using a whip stitch. Stop when you have sewn three sides together. Then stuff the pillow with polyfill. Stuff it firmly, making sure the stuffing is even and pushed into the corners. Sew up the last side to close the pillow. Tie a knot in the corner, cut off the extra yarn, and hide the end by weaving it into the crocheted rows.

8 Now make pom-poms for the corners if you want to add something extra. Pick a color yarn and wrap it around a ruler about 50 times.

continued on next page

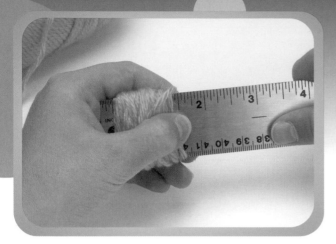

9 Carefully slide the bundle of yarn off the ruler. Hold it with your fingers to keep the loops together.

10 Cut another piece of yarn about 12 inches long. Tie this piece around the middle of the bundle. Pull tightly and tie a knot. It's helpful to have someone help you tie the knot while you hold the bundle.

11 Use scissors to cut all of the loops in the bundle to make the pom-pom. Trim the ends to shape the pom-pom. Be sure to leave the ends of the yarn used to tie the knot around the pom-pom bundle.

12 Use the long ends of the yarn to tie the pom-pom onto one corner of the pillow. Thread one end through the stitches of the pillow and tie a knot to hold. Weave the ends through the stitching to hide and cut off the extra yarn.

crochet creatures

these quirky creatures look hard to make, but they're not. You simply crochet a rectangle, stuff it, and sew it closed. Easy! Glue buttons on for eyes. Tie on a bow or collar, or try gluing felt on for a nose or mouth. It's your creature to design any way you want!

BROWN CAT

While called "brown cat," this cat can be any color you want. Make a cat in colors that resemble your little kitty or your best friend's cat. If you want to be adventurous, try crocheting with a novelty textured yarn, like an eyelash yarn, to give your crochet cat a furry look.

materials

- 1 skein worsted weight yarn
- Size I (9) crochet hook
- Polyfill stuffing
- Yarn needle
- Scissors
- 2 buttons for eyes
- Fabric glue

1 Make a slipknot near the end of the yarn and make chain 21 stitches (see page 21). To start your first row, insert the hook into the second stitch from the hook and make 20 single crochet stitches (see pages 22–25), one for each chain stitch. Make a chain stitch at the end of the row.

2 Turn the work over and begin the next row, making 20 single crochet stitches across. Don't forget the chain stitch at the end of the row. Continue crocheting rows until you have a long rectangle (about 64 rows). This will be folded in half to make the cat.

3 Cut the end of the yarn about 6 inches from the last stitch. Pull the end of the yarn through the last stitch to finish, pulling tight. Use a yarn needle to weave the end of the yarn into the rows to hide. Cut off the extra yarn.

4 Fold the rectangle in half.

5 Cut off a long piece of yarn to sew up the sides and thread onto a yarn needle. Tie the end to one of the corners.

6 Sew around the edges using a whip stitch (see page 29), but leave an opening big enough to stuff.

7 Stuff the cat with polyfill until it feels firm.

8 Finish sewing up the side.

continued on next page

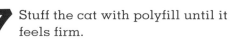

9 To make the ears, thread a piece of yarn on a yarn needle. Insert the needle through a corner to make a few stitches diagonally across the corner. Make sure you're sewing through both layers.

10 Finish on the back side. Make sure both ends of yarn are on this side. Take both ends and pull to cinch up the stitches to form the ear. Tie a knot with the ends.

11 To make the legs, make a few stitched through both layers in the center of the bottom of the cat.

12 Use fabric glue to attach buttons onto the front for eyes.

LOUD-MOUTH CREATURE

Your crocheted creations don't have to resemble real animals! This little guy looks like some kind of weird alien with a gigantic mouth. Let your imagination go to town and have some fun.

materials

- 1 skein of purple and 1 skein of pink worsted weight yarn
- Size I (9) crochet hook
- Polyfill stuffing
- Yarn needle
- Scissors
- 2 buttons for eyes
- Fabric glue

1 Start with the color you want the body to be. Make a slipknot near the end of the yarn and make 21 chain stitches (see page 21). To start your first row, insert the hook into the second stitch from the hook and make 20 single crochet stitches (see pages 22–25), one for each chain stitch. Make a chain stitch at the end of the row.

2 Turn the work over and begin the next row, making 20 single crochet stitches across. Don't forget the chain stitch at the end of the row. Continue crocheting rows until you have a rectangle (about 26 rows). At the end of the 26th row, change to the yarn for the mouth color. (See steps 2–7 of the Striped Scarf project, on pages 69–70, for more about changing yarn colors.)

3 Crochet 6 rows with the new color.

continued on next page

4 Cut the end of the yarn about 6 inches from the last stitch. Pull the end of the yarn through the last stitch at the end of the row to finish, pulling tight. Use a yarn needle to weave the loose ends of the yarns into the rows to hide. Cut off the extra yarn.

5 Lay the piece flat with the pink stripe on top. The finished piece should look like this.

6 Fold the stripe down.

7 Fold the purple edge up to meet the stripe.

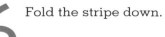

8 Cut a long piece of yarn the color of the body. Tie it to connect both sections.

9 Use a yarn needle to sew the seam shut with a whip stitch (see page 29).

10 The finished piece should look like a tube.

11 Sew up one side. Stuff the creature with polyfill until it's firm. Then sew up the other side.

12 Follow steps 9–12 of the Brown Cat project on page 104 to finish.

matching colors

a color wheel is a tool that helps you mix and match colors. It's very easy to use, and comes in handy when you want colors to pop and stand out in your crochet projects. Simply point to a color on the wheel. Then move your finger directly across the wheel to the opposite color. In seconds you have what is called a complimentary color, or a color that contrasts.

For example, say your favorite color is blue, and you want to crochet a project with blue yarn and would like a contrasting color. Point to the blue slice on the color wheel. Now, move your finger directly across the wheel. You'll see that orange is a perfect complimentary color for blue. How easy was that! Play around with all of the colors and see which of your favorite colors compliment each other.

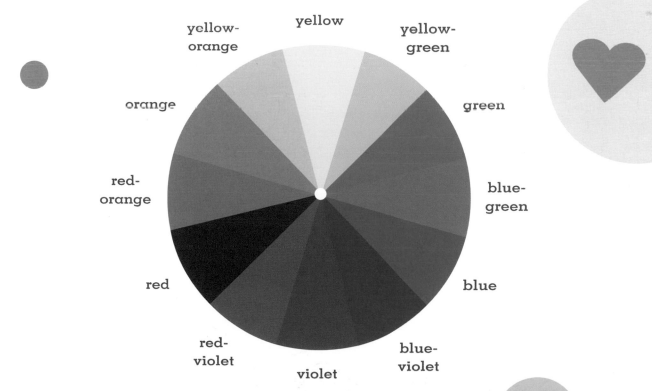

yellow-orange
yellow
yellow-green
orange
green
red-orange
blue-green
red
blue
red-violet
blue-violet
violet

project journal

Use this page to keep a journal of your crochet projects. Fill in the type and color of yarn you chose, the materials you used, the kind of stitches you made, and if you gave it as a gift—or made it for yourself!

Crochet Project:
Type of Yarn:
Color of Yarn:
Other Materials:
Stitches:
Use:

Crochet Project:
Type of Yarn:
Color of Yarn:
Other Materials:
Stitches:
Use:

Crochet Project:
Type of Yarn:
Color of Yarn:
Other Materials:
Stitches:
Use:

Crochet Project:
Type of Yarn:
Color of Yarn:
Other Materials:
Stitches:
Use:

Crochet Project:
Type of Yarn:
Color of Yarn:
Other Materials:
Stitches:
Use:

Crochet Project:
Type of Yarn:
Color of Yarn:
Other Materials:
Stitches:
Use:

Crochet Project:
Type of Yarn:
Color of Yarn:
Other Materials:
Stitches:
Use:

Crochet Project:
Type of Yarn:
Color of Yarn:
Other Materials:
Stitches:
Use:

Crochet Project:
Type of Yarn:
Color of Yarn:
Other Materials:
Stitches:
Use:

Crochet Project:
Type of Yarn:
Color of Yarn:
Other Materials:
Stitches:
Use:

INDEX